Denman's Handbook
For Auto Mechanics
And Technicians

Denman's Handbook For Auto Mechanics And Technicians

Ernest Denman

To order additional copies of this book, contact:
Xlibris Corporation
1-888-795-4274
www.Xlibris.com
Orders@Xlibris.com
96876

Contents

ABOUT THE AUTHOR

Early in his career, Ernest Denman went to work as an apprentice for a large utility company in Houston, Texas, which had a very large fleet of cars, trucks, hydraulic equipment, trailers, cranes, and heavy equipment. The apprentice program helped young men and women to enter the work force by learning new skills. Jumping at the chance to work and start a family, he went for their training program, which taught the fundamentals and more. Not only did Ernest get the basic training in electrical systems, he learned hydraulics, transmissions, gears, instrumentation, and even built engines!

The turning point in his life came when a supervisor advised that the day of the shade tree mechanic was ending. Success depended on the ability to use technical information and learning all of the tools and safety procedures. Yes, there was a time when one could go tinker and learn how to fix that old car that is in the front yard or driveway. But, the question was, would you be able to make a good living?

Ernest took the advice to heart. He has a deep commitment to helping others to build rewarding careers as skilled mechanics.

INTRODUCTION

If you are serious about becoming consistently better at your craft, you will benefit from this book. Whether your mechanical specialty is automotive electrical systems, hydraulics, or gasoline and diesel engine, my hope is that this quick reference handbook will become a vital tool in your toolbox. My career began when I joined a three-year apprentice program. Now, I have grown into a highly skilled mechanic, ready to share my knowledge and experience. This compilation of what I have learned throughout my years of experience as a mechanic technician will help to build on your fundamental knowledge and provide insight into how to do your job better.

The better your skill level with a wide variety of tools, the more money you will make on a wider variety of jobs. Be open to learning how to use everything, from hand tools, meters, gauges, and torches to computers, and even iPads.

Study the new technology and become proficient. Learning to read electrical, hydraulic, and welding schematics will allow you to quickly troubleshoot equipment, accurately diagnose components, and complete any job with quality and confidence. And remember, a highly skilled mechanic technician always works safely.

ACKNOWLEDGEMENT

I would like to extend a personal thank you toward my loving wife (Pat), who has patiently supported me through the first of my writing endeavors.

Also, I am thankful to my "sounding board" and chief editor, Marilyn Howard Jones, who has graciously provided insight and counseling throughout my publishing process.

CENTIGRADE/FAHRENHEIT EQUIVALENCIES

Use the following as a guide for calculations.

Converting Between °C and °F
$(°C \times 9/5) + 32 = °F$
$(°F - 32) \times 5/9 = °C$

Centigrade/Fahrenheit Quick Reference Table

Centigrade	Fahrenheit	Centigrade	Fahrenheit	Centigrade	Fahrenheit	Centigrade	Fahrenheit
0	32	27	80.6	54	129.2	81	177.8
2	35.6	29	84.2	56	132.8	83	181.4
5	41	32	89.6	59	138.2	86	186.8
7	44.6	34	93.2	61	141.8	88	190.4
8	46.4	35	95	62	143.6	89	192.2
10	50	37	98.6	64	147.2	91	195.8
17	62.6	44	111.2	71	160.8	98	208
19	66.2	46	114.8	73	164.4	100	212
20	68	47	116.6	74	166.2	101	213.8
21	69.8	48	118.4	75	168	102	215.6
23	73.4	50	122	77	170.6	104	219.2
24	77	52	125.6	79	174.2	106	222.8
26	78.8	53	127.4	80	176	107	224.6

*The *degree Fahrenheit (°F)* non-metric temperature scale was devised and evolved over time so that the freezing and boiling temperatures of water are whole numbers, but not round numbers as in the Celsius temperature scale.

*The *degree Celsius (°C)* scale was devised by dividing the range of temperature between the freezing and boiling temperatures of pure water at standard atmospheric conditions (sea level pressure) into one hundred equal parts. Temperatures on this scale were at one time known as degrees centigrade; however, it is no longer correct to use that terminology. The 9th General Conference on Weights and Measures (CGPM) changed the official name from "centigrade degree" to "Celsius degree" in 1948.

British Thermal Unit (BTU) and Calorie

BTU	Calorie
A British Thermal Unit is the amount of heat required to raise the temperature of one pound of water, one degree Fahrenheit.	A Calorie is the amount of heat required to raise the temperature of one cubic centimeter of water one degree of centigrade.
One BTU (approximately) is Calorie × 252.016	One gram calorie (approximately) is BTU × 0.003968

It is very useful to know how to calculate the heat value in gasoline. A gallon of gasoline produces approximately 19,000 BTUs. When used as a unit of power, BTU per hour (BTU/h) is the actual unit, though this is often abbreviated as BTU.

Gasoline/1 gallon = Approximately 115,000 to 124,000 BTU/gallon

No 2 diesel/1 gallon = Approximately 138,000 to 140,000 BTU/gallon

Example: 2.2 gallons of gasoline × 19,000 = 38,000 BTU

When converting one gallon of gasoline to calories burned, you need to know how many grams make up a gallon of gasoline. One gallon =3,785 × 0.70 grams per milliliter = grams

Example: 1 × 3,785 × 0.70 = 2,650 grams. Thus 2,650 grams × 0.003968 BTU = 10.5152 calories

A gallon of gasoline will usually contain from 115,000 to 125,000 BTUs. Most technicians want the gasoline with the most BTUs, which can be misleading. The BTU content is of little value if some of the gasoline is still burning when the exhaust valve opens and all of that energy escapes out of the exhaust as heat and unburned hydrocarbons. Most engines that exceed 7,000 rpm can benefit more from an 115,000 BTU per gallon gasoline than a heavier gasoline that may contain 125,000 BTUs per gallon, but does not have time to completely burn in the combustion chamber.

Think about this: One gasoline has 115,000 BTUs and is 95 percent burned before the exhaust valve opens; the other contains 125,000 BTUs but is only 85 percent burned before the exhaust valve opens. Simple math tells us that the first gasoline gave up 109,250 BTUs. The other gave up 106,250 BTUs.

Which would you prefer? I would take the 109,250 BTUs from the 115,000 BTU per gallon gasoline. Does this actually happen? Sure it does. Although some heat energy does go out the exhaust, generally, more BTUs burn more horsepower. However, higher BTUs do not necessarily mean the engine will generate the most horse power on that particular engine.

COMPARING UNITS OF MEASUREMENTS WITH U.S. STANDARD MEASURES

The following tables contain basic information about the units of measure used in the United States—linear measurements, square area, dry volume, cubic volume, and weight.

Linear Equivalencies					
Mile	Furlong	Rod	Yard	Feet	Inch
1	8	160	1,760	5,280	
	1	40	220	660	
		1	5.5	16.5	198
			1	3	36
				1	12

Square Area Equivalencies						
Township	Square mile	Acre	Square rod	Square yard	Square feet	Square inch
1	36					
	1	640				
		1	160	4,840		
			1	30.25	272.25	
				1	9	
					1	144

Dry Volume Equivalencies			
Bushel	Peck	Quart	Pint
1	4	32	
	1	8	16
		1	2

Liquid Volume Equivalencies								
Drum Oil	Barrel	Gallon	Quart	Pint	Cup	Ounce	Tablespoon	Teaspoon
1		55						
	1	42						
		1	4	8	16	128		
			1	2	4	32		
				1	2	16		
					1	8		
						1	3	
							1	3

Cubic Yard Equivalencies				
Pounds of water	No. of gallons	Cubic feet	Cubic yards	Cubic inches
8.34	1			231
62.38	7.48	1		1,728
1,684		27	1	

Weight Equivalencies				
Ton	Hundred Weight	Pound	Ounce	Troy Ounce
t	cwt	lb	oz	Tr.ozt
1	20	2,000		
	1	100		
		1	16	12

Metric Standards

Linear							
Kilometer	Hectometer	Decameter	Meter	Decimeter	Centimeter	Millimeter	Micron
km	hm	dam	m	dm	cm	mm	µm
1	10	100	1,000				
	1	10	100				
		1	10				
			1	10	100	1,000	1,000,000
				1	10	100	100,000
					1	10	10,000
						1	1,000

Cubic Volume

Cubic meter	Decimeter	Cubic yard	Cubic millimeter
1	1,000		
	1	1,000	1,000,000
		1	1,000
	One cubic decimeter is also a liter	One cubic centimeter is also a milliliter	
One cubic meter of water is also a metric ton	One cubic decimeter of water is also a kilogram	One cubic centimeter of water is also a gram	One cubic millimeter of water is also a milligram

Weight

Metric ton	Kilogram	Gram	Milligram
1	1,000		
	1	1,000	1,000,000
		1	1,000
One metric ton of water is a cubic meter	One kilogram of water is a cubic decimeter—also known as a liter	One gram of water is a cubic decimeter—also known as a milliliter	One milligram of water is also a cubic millimeter

Square Area

Square kilometer	Square meter	Square decimeter	Square centimeter	Square millimeter
1	1,000,000			
	1	100	10,000	
		1	11	10,000
				100

Lenght

inches × 25.4 = mm inches × 2.54 = cm inches × 254 = m	feet × 0.3048 = m yards × 0.9144 = m miles × 1.609 = km
km × 0.62137 = miles m × 1.0936143 = yards m × 3.2808429 = feet	m × 39.37011 = inches cm × 0.3937011 = inches mm × 0.03937011 = inches

Volume

cubic yard × 0.76455 = cubic meter cubic feet × 28.316735 = 1 cubic inch × 0.016387 = 1	cubic meter × 1.30796 = cubic yard liter × 0.035315 = cubic feet liter × 61.024 = cubic inches

Area

square miles × 2.5899 = square kilometer acres × 0.0040467 = square kilometer	square kilometer × 0.38611 = square miles square kilometer × 247.1104 = acres

Fluid Volume

gallon × 3.7854 = liter quart × 0.94634 = liter ounce × 0.02958 = liter	liter × 0.264175 = gallons liter × 1.0567 = quarts liter × 33.8 = ounces
ounce × 29.58 = milliliter	milliliter × 0.0338 = ounces

Weight

ounces × 28.3495 = grams	gram × 0.035274 = ounces
pounds × 0.45358 = kilograms	kilograms × 2.204622 = pounds
U.S. tons × 0.90718 = metric ton	metric tons × 1.1023 = U.S. tons

Heat

°F − 32° × 0.555555 = °C	°C × 1.8 + 32° = °F
BTU × 252.27 = Calorie	Calorie × 0.003964 = BTU

Pressure

psi × 6.9 = kPa	kPa × 0.1449 = psi

Decimal to Millimeter Conversion

Use this chart to quickly convert a decimal inch dimension to millimeter.

Decimal to Millimeter Conversion Table

1st position		2nd position		3rd position		4th position	
Inch	mm	Inch	mm	Inch	mm	Inch	mm
.1	2.54	.01	.254	.001	.0254	.0001	.00254
.2	5.08	.02	.508	.002	.0508	.0002	.00508
.3	7.62	.03	.762	.003	.0762	.0003	.00762
.4	10.16	.04	1.016	.004	.1016	.0004	.01016
.5	12.70	.05	1.270	.005	.1270	.0005	.01270
.6	15.24	.06	1.524	.006	.1524	.0006	.01524
.7	17.78	.07	1.778	.007	.1778	.0007	.01778
.8	20.32	.08	2.032	.008	.2032	.0008	.02032
.9	22.86	.09	2.286	.009	.2286	.0009	.02286

Note: The decimal is always in a straight line.

Example
Refer to the chart to convert 0.125 to mm. Using the table, 0.1 is in the first position; 2 is in the second position; 5 is in the third position; and 0 is in the fourth position. Add the decimals. The result is 3.1750 mm.

4th position = 0.0000

3rd position = 0.1270

2nd position = 0.508

1st position = 2.54

Sum = 3.1750 mm

Decimal to Millimeter Conversion

Use the following method for conversion by multiplying.

Multiply 11.090 inches times 25.4, and the product will equal millimeters.

Example (Refer to page 12)

Convert 11.090 inches to millimeters
$11.090'' \times 25.4 = 281.686$ mm

U.S. Standard Gauge for Iron and Steel

When ordering sheet metal, knowing the dimensions is important. Use these tables and formulas for quick calculations.

Sheet Metal Dimensions

Gauge	Fraction	Decimal
28	1/64	.015625
22	1/32	.03125
16	1/16	.0625
14	5/64	.078125
13	3/32	.09375
12	7/64	.109375
11	1/8	.125
10	9/64	.140625
9	5/32	.15625
8	11/64	.171875

Sheet Metal Plate Dimensions

Gauge	Fraction	Decimal
7	3/16	.1875
6	13/64	.2344
3	¼	.2500
2	17/64	.2656
1	9/32	.2812
0	5/16	.3125
00	11/32	.3438
000	3/8	.3750
0000	13/32	.4063
00000	7/16	.4375
000000	15/32	.4688

Systematic Instructions for Estimating the Weight of Steel

Bar stock: Multiply the width times the thickness (in inches). Multiply that product times 10 and then divide that by 3. The result is the approximate weight in pounds per foot of length.

Example: 8 (feet) × 0.5 (inch) = 4.0 × 10/3 = 13.3 lb

Plate:

By square inch: Multiply the square inches of the plate by the thickness (in inches). Then multiply that number by 0.278 and the result is the approximate weight in pounds.

Example: 576 (square inches) × 0.25 (thick) = 144 × 0.278 = 40 lb

By square foot: Multiply the square footage of the plate by the thickness (in inches). Then multiply that number by 40 and the result is the approximate weight in pounds. Example: 2 × length × 2 × width = square feet

Example:

3 (feet) × 2 (feet) = 6 ft

6 ft × 0.25 thick = 1.5 × 40 = 60 lb

Round stock: Multiply the diameters (in inches) times four and then square the product. Divide that number by six and the result is the approximate weight in pounds per foot of length.

Example: 0.50 (inches) × 4 = 2.0 squared = 2.0 × 2.0 = 4.0/6 = 1.5 lb

Square stock: Square the thickness (in inches) and multiply that times ten. Divide the result by three and that equals the approximate weight in pounds per foot of length.

Example: 1 × 10 = 10/3 = 3.3 lb

Working with an Internal Combustion Engines

When rebuilding an engine, you will need to know the size of the cylinder. There are certain specifications that have to stay within tolerance.

Definitions

Bore—The diameter of cylinder in the engine.

Stroke—The distance that the piston moves from bottom dead center (BDC) to top dead center (TDC). This travel is determined entirely by the crankshaft.

Displacement—The volume of air moved by a piston during its stroke, times the number of cylinders in the engine equals the engine displacement. This is shown as cubic inches displacement (CID) or liter (L).

Essential Formulas

Cylinder Displacement—Divide the bore by two, to find the radius. Square the radius and multiply it times Pi, 3.1416. Multiply that by the stroke equals cylinder displacement.

Engine Displacement—Multiply the cylinder displacement times the number of cylinders.

Compression Ratio—The comparison of the total volume of one cylinder with the piston at BDC and combustion chamber volume, the piston at TDC.

Example:

Combustion chamber = 2 cu. in.

1 cylinder displacement = 36 cu. in.

Volume of cylinder = 38 cu. in.
The total volume, 38 cu. in., divided by the combustion chamber volume, 2 cu. in., equals 38/2. This can be expressed as 19:1.

Formula

To find L, multiply CID × 61.024 = L
To find CID, multiply L × 0.016387 = CID

Displacement Equivalence Table

Liter	CID	Liter	CID	Liter	CID	Liter	CID
1.9	116	3.1	191	5.0	305	7.0	427
2.3	140	3.8	231	5.3	327	7.3	447
2.5	153	4.1	250	5.9	360	7.5	460

TORQUE WRENCH ADAPTORS

If you have to use an adaptor with a torque wrench, the adaptor length will affect the amount of torque applied to the fastener. The following formula will allow you to compute the correct torque wrench reading for the correct amount of torque.

$$T_w = T_a \{L/(L + A)\}$$

Example: $T_w = 60 \{15/[15'' + 6'']\}$

$$T_w = 60\{15/[.21]\}$$

$$T_w = 60 \times 0.71$$

$$T_w = 42.6 \text{ lb. ft.}$$

where T_w = Torque wrench reading (lb. ft.)

T_a = Torque applied to fastener (lb. ft.)

L = Length of torque wrench only (inches)

A = Length of adaptor (inches)

Example:
If the specification calls for 60 foot-pounds of torque and you have to use an adaptor on your torque wrench, what reading should be on the wrench to properly apply 60 foot-pounds to the fastener?

The torque wrench is 15 inches from the center of the handle to the center of the square drive. The adaptor is three inches between the centers of the square drives.

Find:
in. lb: Multiply lb ft × 12 = in. lb

lb ft: Divide in lb by 12 = lb. ft

in. oz: Multiply in lb × 16 = in. oz

in. lb: Divide in oz by 16 = in. lb

STANDARD TORQUE CHART

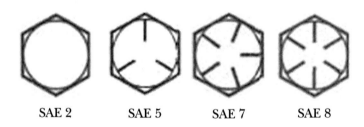

	SAE 2	SAE 5	SAE 7	SAE 8

Grade	2	5	7	8	Socket head cap screw
ID Marks	No markings	3 lines	5 lines	6 lines	Allen head
Material	Low carbon	Medium-carbon, tempered	Medium-carbon, quenched and tempered	Medium-carbon, quenched and tempered	High-carbon, quenched and tempered
Tensile strength (Minimum)	74,000 psi	120,000 psi	133,000 psi	150,000 psi	160,000 psi

U.S. Bolt Torque Specifications
Torque in pounds-foot

Bolt Dia.	Thread per inch	2	2	5	5	7	7	8	8	Socket head cap screw	Socket head cap screw
		Dry	Oiled	Dry	Oiled	Dry	Oiled	Dry	Oiled	Dry	Oiled
1/4	20	4	3	8	6	10	8	12	9	14	11
1/4	28	6	4	10	7	12	9	14	10	16	13
5/16	18	9	7	17	13	21	16	25	18	29	23
5/16	24	12	9	19	14	24	18	29	20	33	26
3/8	16	16	12	30	23	40	30	45	35	49	39
3/8	24	22	16	35	25	45	35	50	40	54	44
7/16	14	24	17	50	35	60	45	70	55	76	61
7/16	20	34	26	55	40	70	50	80	60	85	68
1/2	13	38	31	75	55	95	70	110	80	113	90
1/2	20	52	42	90	65	100	80	120	90	126	100
9/16	12	52	42	110	80	135	100	150	110	163	130
9/16	18	71	57	120	90	150	110	170	130	181	144
5/8	11	98	78	150	110	140	190	220	170	230	184
5/8	18	115	93	180	130	210	160	240	180	255	204
3/4	10	157	121	260	200	320	240	380	280	400	320
3/4	16	180	133	300	220	360	280	420	320	440	350
7/8	9	210	160	430	320	520	400	600	460	640	510
7/8	14	230	177	470	360	580	440	660	500	700	560
1	8	320	240	640	480	800	600	900	680	980	780
1	12	350	265	710	530	860	666	990	740	1060	845

This chart should be used to determine the maximum torque that can be applied to a bolt without damaging the bolt. If the retained part is subject to distortion or any damage from strain, use the reduced torque specified by the part manufacturer.

TENSILE STRENGTH EQUIVALENCY

The class designating tensile strength is shown on each metric stud, bolt, and nut in Arabic numerals. Small metric studs and standard nuts use the marks shown in the chart below.

Stud marks	None	Circle (0)	Cross (+)	Diamond/Square	None
ISO* Class	4.6, 4.8, 5.8	8.8	9.8	10.9	12.9
SAE Nut Marks	None	3 Dots	6 Dots	None	None
SAE Equal	Grade 1–2	Grade 5	Grade 8	None	None

*ISO =International Organization of Standardization, usually uses metric standards.

How to Convert Brinell Hardness to Tensile Strength

Divide the Brinell hardness number by two and then multiply the result by 1,000. The result equals the tensile strength in psi.

Example: Brinell hardness number is 248

Dividing 248 by 2 equals 124

Multiplying 124 times 1,000 equals 124,000

The tensile strength is 124,000

$248/2 = 124 \times 1,000 = 124,000$

Convert Tensile Strength to Brinell Hardness

Divide tensile strength (psi) by 1,000, and then multiply the result by two. The result is the Brinell hardness number.

Example: Tensile strength is 100,000 psi

Dividing 100,000 by 1,000 equals 100

$100,000/1,000 = 100 \times 2 = 200$

Multiplying by two equals 200

The Brinell hardness number is 200

Electrical Equations
Ohm's Law

This law states that the direct current flowing in a conductor is directly proportional to the potential difference between its ends.

To find resistance (R)

$R = V/A$

To find volts (V)

$V = A \times R$

To find amps (A)

$A = V/R$

International Symbols
E = electromotive
I = amps, A
R = resistance, ohms

Power

To find watts (W and kW)

$V \times A = W$

$hp \times 0.746\ kW$

To find horse power (hp):

$W \times 746 \times \text{efficiency percentage} = hp$

$kW \times 1.34048\ \text{efficiency percentage} = hp$

BTU/hour × 2,545 = hp

BTU/min. × 42.44 = hp

T (in pound feet) × rpm/5,252 = hp

To find torque: hp × 5,252/rpm = T (in pound feet)

To find BTU: psi × GPM × 1.5 = BTU

ICC Wiring Color Code, from
Department of Transportation (DOT) Regulations

Red—Stop lights
Green—Right turn lights
Yellow—Left turn lights
Brown—Tail lights
Black—Clearance/marker/ID lights
Blue—Auxiliary lights

Electrical Brake Controls Color Code

Black—Battery
Red—Cold side of stoplight switch
Blue or grey—Return to six-way trailer plug (brake wire)

QUICK GUIDE TO GEOMETRIC CONVERSIONS

Finding Dimensions—The Circle

As the skill level increases, the welder becomes a fabricator. This quick reference can be used by the welder technician during fabricating and helps with determining dimension.

Circumference
1. Multiply the diameter times 3.1416, or
2. Multiply the radius times 6.2832, or
3. Multiply the square root of the circle area by 3.5449

Area
Multiply 3.1416 times the radius squared, or
Multiply the diameter squared times 0.7854, or
Multiply the circumference squared times 0.07958

Length of an Area
Multiply the degrees of the arc times the radius times 0.0174533

Radius
1. Divide the diameter by 2, or
2. Multiply the circumference times 0.15916,
3. Multiply the square root of the area times 0.56419

Diameter
1. Multiply the radius times 2, or
2. Multiply circumference times 0.31831, or
3. Multiply the square root of the area times 1.1284

Area of a Sector
1. Multiply the radius times the length of the arc, and then divide by 2

Finding the Area of Other Common Shapes

Hexagon
1. Multiply the square of the distance across times 0.86603, or
2. Multiply the area of the inscribed circle by 1.1027

Octagon
1. Multiply the square of the distance across times 0.82843, or
2. Multiply the area of the inscribed circle by 1.0548

Rectangle
1. Multiply the length times the width

Triangle
1. Multiply the length of the base times half of the perpendicular height

The Right Triangle

$$a^2 + b^2 = c^2.$$

The Pythagorean Theorem states that the square of the hypotenuse of a right triangle equals the sum of the square of the length of the other two sides. This formula can be used to make a number of determinations.

Finding the length of an unknown side and making a right angle

Example 1: Finding an unknown length is a right triangle.

Let length of hypotenuse = 100 and length of one side = 60.
Then length of other side = ?

The square of the hypotenuse equals 10,000. Subtract the square of the known side, 3,000, and that leaves 6,400. The square root of 6,400 is 80, the length of the third side.

Example 2: Finding a 90° angle

1. Measure three feet from a point.
2. Measure four feet from the same point at approximately 90°.

3. The angle between these two lines will be 90° when the distance between the far points is five feet.

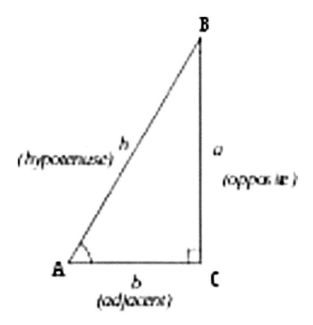

Note: Any combination of distances in the same relationship of 3:4:5 will achieve the same result. For instance, multiply each distance by twenty to get 60:80:100. Making a triangle with these three distances will also produce the right angle.

CAPACITY OF A CYLINDER

Cylindrical Tank

Multiply the length in inches times the square area of the circular base.

Example: Length is 36″ and the diameter is 18″

18-inch diameter divided by two equals 9-inch radius
9-inch radius squared is 81
81 times Pi (3.1416) equals 254.47 sq. in.
254.47 sq. in. times 36 inches length equals 9,161 cu. in.
9,160.9 cu. in. divided by 1,728 equals 6.3 cu. in.

Rectangular Tank

Multiply the length in inches, times the depth in inches, times the width in inches.

Example: The tank is 10″ by 16″ by 12″
10 × 16 × 12 = 1,920 cu. in.
1,920 cu. in. divided by 1,728 = 1.1 cu. ft.

Elliptical Tank

Multiply the length in inches, times the short diameter in inches, times the long diameter in inches. Multiply this product times 0.0034, and the result is in gallons.

Example: The tank is 36 inches long. The long diameter is 20 inches, and the short diameter is 7 inches.
36 times 20 × 7 = 5,040
5,040 × 0.0034 = 17.14 gallons

Conical Tank

Multiply the altitude of the cone in inches times the area of the base in square inches. Multiply this by 1/3 for the cubic inches.

Example: The cone is 116 inches in diameter and 72 inches tall.

116 diameters divided by 2 equals 58 inches radius
58 times 58 times 3.1416 equal 10,568.342 sq. in.
10,568.342 times 72 inches equals 760,920.62
760,920.62 multiplied by 1/3 equal 253,640.2 cu. in.
253,640.2 divided by 1,728 equals 146.78 cu. in.

To find gallons—one cubic foot has 1,728 cu. in. Divide the cubic inches by 231 and the result is gallons.

Example: How many gallons in 2½ cu. ft.?

Multiply 1,728 times 2.5 cu. ft. equals 4,320 cu. in. Divide 4,320 cu. in. by 231. This equals 18.7 gallons.

Hydraulics

Thrust from a cylinder
   $T = A \times P$
   $A = T/P$
   $P = T/A$

A = Surface area of piston
T = Cylinder thrust
P = Hydraulic pressure
F = Effective force
a = Least angle, in degrees, between

Cylinder Axis and Load Direction

To find power:
   BTU/hour × 42.44 = hp
   Torque (in pound feet) × rpm/5,252 = hp
   psi × GPM/1,714 × efficiency percentage = hp

Approximate HP:
   1 GPM at 1,500 psi requires 1 hp

To find Torque:
   hp × 5,252/rpm = Torque (in pound feet)

To find BTU:
   psi × GPM × 1.5 = BTU

Before disconnecting and installing hydraulics attachments to a machine. The technician has to install wiring, hoses in the right position. As you view these photos some connections can be complicated.

Boyle's Law:

The absolute pressure of a confined body of gas varies inversely as its volume, provided its temperature remains constant.

$$P_1 \times V_1 = P_2 \times V_2 \text{ or } PV = c$$

Note: Boyle's law applies to most gases, under 1,000 psi, and with pressure reading in absolute.

Charles' Law:

If the temperature of a gas increases, its volume increases in the same ratio if the pressure remains the same.

$$T_1 \times P_2 = T_2 \times P_1$$

Or, if the temperature of a gas increases, its pressure increases in the same ratio if the volume remains the same.

$$T_1 \times V_2 = T_2 \times V_1$$

Pascal's Law:

Pressure set up in a confined body of fluid disperse equally in all directions, and always at right angles to the containing surfaces.

REGULATING OXYGEN/ACETYLENE PRESSURE

Tip Size and Pressure Selection

Inches	Tip size	Speed *IPM	Oxygen PSIG	Acetylene PSIG	Kerfs Width
1/8	000	28–32	20–25	3–5	.04
¼	00	27–30	20–25	3–5	.05
3/8	0	24–28	25–30	3–5	.06
½	0	20–24	30–35	3–5	.06
¾	1	17–21	30–35	3–5	.07
1	2	15–19	35–40	3–6	.09
1½	2	13–17	40–45	3–7	.09
2	3	12–15	40–45	4–8	.11
2½"	3	10–13	45–50	4–10	.11
3	4	9–12	40–50	5–10	.12
4	5	8–11	45–55	5–12	.15
5	5	7–9	50–55	5–13	.15
6	6	6–8	45–55	7–13	.18
8	6	5–6	45–55	7–14	.19
10	7	4–5	45–55	10–15	.34
12	8	3–5	45–55	10–15	.41

*IPM—Minimum and maximum inches per minute

Notes: Speeds and pressure settings applied may vary based on types of steel.

Estimating gas consumption is based upon oxygen being used at 1.1 times the rate of acetylene for a neutral flame. It can still vary greatly depending upon the metal and the particular skill of the operator.

The pressures on this chart are measured at the regulator using a ¼" hose, and also with the length of the hose at 25 feet and a No5 tip or smaller. If a larger tip or longer hose is used, the hose size may change or be increased to 3/8 inch.

Safety Caution

At no time should the withdrawal pressure of acetylene exceed 15 psi. If the withdrawal rate needs to exceed 1/7 of a cylinder per hour, use an acetylene manifold system of sufficient size to supply the necessary volume.

Before welding, you must clean surfaces,
consider placement and fabricate your work piece.

Before welding , you must clean surfaces,
consider placement and fabricate your work piece.

Your piece will be fabricated and fitted.

Your piece will be fabricated and fitted.

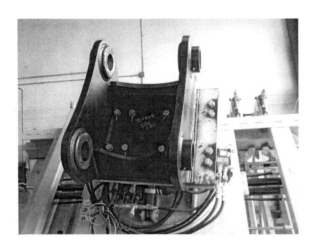

The end result is clean weld and nice fabricated piece that fits.

AMERICAN WELDING SOCIETY CLASSIFICATION SYSTEM

A welder performs manual, machine, automatic, or semiautomatic welding operation.

Typical AWA electrode code: **E-6011**
"E" = Electrode
60 = Tensile strength of weld number times 1,000. Example: 60 × 1,000 = 60,000 pound per square inch.
1 = The third number represents welding positions. 3 = flat only (F), 2 = flat and horizontal (F and H), 1 = all positions including vertical and overhead.
1 = The fourth number represents coating on electrode and welding characteristics. See the chart below.

Some Electrode Operation Characteristics, Fourth Digit

Digit	Coating	Welding current	Characteristics
0	Cellulose Sodium	DCR	Deep penetration, flat or concave beads, fast fill
1	Cellulose Potassium	AC, DCR	Deep penetration flat or concave beads, fast fill
2	Titania Sodium	AC, DCR	Medium penetration convex beads full freeze
3	Titania Potassium	AC, DCR, DCS	Shallow penetration convex beads fill freeze
4	Titania Iron powder	AC, DCR DCS	Medium penetration fast deposit fill freeze fast freeze*
5	Low hydrogen	DCR	Moderate penetration convex beads welding high sulfur and high carbon steels
6	Low hydrogen	AC DCR	Moderate penetration convex beads welding high sulfur and high carbon steel
7	Iron power Iron oxide	AC DCR DCS	Medium penetration flat bead fast freeze
8	Iron powder Low hydrogen	AC DCR	Shallow to medium penetration convex bead fill freeze

*Fast-freeze rods: These rods have the ability to cool rapidly even while the weld process is in motion.

Selection of Electrodes for Welding

Fast-freeze rods have the ability to cool rapidly even while the weld process is in motion.

Characteristic	Welding position	AWS class Rods	Primary polarity	Alternate polarity	Rod size inches	Amp Current range	Volt range
Deep penetration, fast freeze, thin slag, can use whipping motion. Metal prep not critical	All positions. Best use on vertical, V, and overhead	E-6010	DCR		3/32	50–90	15–17
					1/8	80–120	17–20
					5/32	110–160	18–21
					3/16	150–200	21–22
		E-6011	AC	DCR	3/32	50–90	15–17
					1/8	80–130	17–20
					5/32	120–180	18–21
					3/16	140–220	21–22

Fill-freeze electrodes fill up a joint quickly as well as solidify quickly.

Characteristics	Welding position	AWS class	Primary polarity	Alternate polarity	Rod size inches
Moderate forceful arc, lower rate of deposition than fast freeze, easy arc start, dense slag, complete coverage, smooth bead, good fillet profile, quite arc slight spatter, medium penetration.	All positions. But best for flat and overhead.	E-6012	DCS	AC	3/32 1/8 5/32 3/16

Characteristic	Welding position	AWS class rods	Primary polarity	Alternate polarity	Rod size diameter		
Moderate forceful arc, lower rate of deposition than fast freeze, easy start and easy to maintain arc with smaller diameter rods. Bead smoother and flatter than E-6012 heavy slag, low penetration.	All positions. But best for flat and overhead	E-6013			3/32 1/8 5/32 3/16	30–80 80–120 120–190 140–240	15–17 17–20 18–21 21–22

Low hydrogen is suitable for all positions on hardened steels where no preheat is used and on cold rolled steels normally exhibiting excessive porosity when welded with conventional rod. The low hydrogen content reduces cracking.

Characteristic	Welding position	AWS class rods	Primary polarity	Alternate polarity	Rod size diameter		
Medium penetration, convex bead, flat fillets, resist cracking, medium to long arc will cause porosity. Note: E-7016 1/8 rod and smaller will tend to stick when using AC. Metal prep is critical	All position: horizontal, flat, vertical, and overhead	E-7015	DCR		3/32 1/8 5/32 3/16		
	All positions	E-7016					
Good penetration, heavy slag, smooth quite arc, very low spatter, adequate penetration at high travel speed, high deposition. Metal prep is critical	All positions: horizontal, flat, vertical, and overhead.	E-7018			3/32 1/8 5/32 3/16	70–120 100–150 120–200 200–275	15–17 17–20 18–21 21–22

Selecting a Rod Size

Base metal thickness inch	Electrode size diameter
1/16–1/8	3/32
1/8–1/4	1/8
1/4–3/8	1/8, 5/32
3/8–1/2	1/8, 5/32, 3/16
1/2–3/4	3/16, 7/32
3/4–1"	1/4

TROUBLESHOOTING GUIDE FOR WELDERS

Arc blow

Magnetic field set up by DC welding current deflects the arc from its proper path. Use an AC machine. Use a very short arc and point the electrode in the direction of the blow. Relocate the ground connection or use two ground cables. Use a nonmagnetic backup strip or nonmagnetic plate as a ground.

Arc is hard to start

Check for the following:

1.) Current setting too low
2.) Flux covered electrode
3.) Work not properly cleaned
4.) Work not properly grounded

Cracked welds

1.) Incorrect size and/or shape of bead
Solution: Adjust size of puddle and speed of travel in keeping with the weight of the welded section.
2.) Faulty design and/or pre-weld preparation of joint.
Solution: Remove weld and clean with gouging rod or plasma cutter
3.) Rigidity of structure
Solution: Preheat and post-heat use skip back or other welding technique to prevent build up of stresses.
4.) Wrong electrode
Solution: Match electrode to metal and or job.

5.) Too rapid cooling of weld deposit
Solution: Preheat and post-heat use non-ferrous electrode. On alloy steel, use austenitic rather air hardening deposit.

Excessive Spatter
Check for the following:

1.) Current setting too high.
2.) Holding too long an arc
3.) Arc blow
4.) Incorrect polarity for electrode being used. Select proper electrode or polarity.

Excessive Convexity
Check for the following:

1.) Current too low
2.) Travel speed too slow

Overlap
Check for the following:

1.) Improper electrode angle
2.) Arc length too long

Porosity
Check for the following:

1.) Incorrect current setting.
2.) Excessive speed of travel or wind blowing shielding gas away.
Solution:
Block wind to prevent losing shielding gases and adjust travel to prevent gas entrapment.
3.) Impurities in or on base metal including rust paint and dirt.
Solution: Properly clean and prepare joint for welding; keep penetration at a minimum.
4.) Arc too long
5.) Incorrect electrode angle
6.) Wet electrode
7.) Slag left on weld bead

Poor Fusion
Check for the following:

1.) Current setting too low
2.) Wrong type of electrode
3.) Incorrect electrode manipulation.
   Solution: Adjust electrode weaving and speed. It ensures melting of both sides.
4.) Too long of an arc gap
5.) Improper preparation of work piece for welding beveled and cleaned

Rough Appearance
Check for the following:

1.) Current setting too high or too low
2.) Incorrect manipulation or wrong work angle of electrode
   Solution: Use weaving technique where needed.
3.) Overheated work
   Solution: Allow work to cool between passes.
4.) Incorrect speed of travel
   Solution: Adjust speed so that proper bead contour is formed
5.) Wrong type of electrode, or wrong polarity

Slag Inclusions
Check for the following:

1.) Current setting too low
2.) Arc too short
3.) Incorrect manipulation of electrode.
   Solution: Use correct electrode to work angle so that arc force prevents molten metal from overtaking slag.

Undercutting

1.) Welding current too high
2.) Excessive travel speed
3.) Excessive arc length
4.) Incorrect electrode to work angle
   Solution: Adjust electrode angle so that arc force will "hold" molten metal until undercut fills.

5.) Wrong size electrode
6.) Arc blow

Warping or Distortion
Check for the following:
1.) Incorrect placement of pieces to be joined
Solution: Adjust pieces so that they "warp into position"
2.) Poor structural design
Solution: Redesign to allow for warp
3.) Improper jigging
Solution: Use chill plates, proper clamping, etc.
4.) Overheating
Solution: Use short beads to allow cooling between weld
5.) Incorrect welding procedure
Solution: Use proper bead placement and keep weld deposits at a minimum.

Valleys Between Beads
Check for the following:

1.) Improper bead placement.
Solution: Electrode tip is starting too far from previous bead. It should be placed right on the border of the previous bead.
2.) Improper electrode angle
Solution: Should be tilted so arc is pointing into previous bead at a 10° to 15° angle.
3.) Travel speed is too fast

Craters
Check for the following:

1.) Current is too high
2.) Improper technique pulling electrode out too quickly.
3.) Solution: Either hesitate with a light circular motion before pulling out, or stop early and back weld.

(GMAW), (MAG),(MIG) WELDING

Gas metal arc welding (GMAW), sometimes referred to by its subtypes metal inert gas (MIG) welding or metal active gas (MAG) welding, is a semiautomatic or automatic arc process in which a continuous and consumable wire electrode and a shielding gas are fed through a welding gun. A constant voltage, direct current power source is most commonly used.

Approximate Current for Popular Metals

Wire type	Diameter Inches	Gas	Current Amp
Mild Steel	.030 .035 .045 .052 .062	Argon/Oxygen 75/25 percent	150 165 220 240 275
Stainless	.035 .045 .062	Argon/Oxygen 75/25 percent	170 225 285
Aluminum	.030 .045 .052	Argon 100 percent	95 135 180
Deoxidized Copper	.035 .045 .062	Argon 100 percent	180 210 310
Silicon Bronze	.035 .045 .062	Argon 100 percent	165 205 270

Note: Current may vary depending on different machine.

Approximate Current for Aluminum

Thickness inches	Wire diameter	Gas flow psi	Current amps	Volts
.040	.030	15	40	15
.050	.030	15	50	15
.063	.030	15	60	15
.093	.030	15	90	15
.250	3/64	35	220	25
.375	1/16	40	270	26
.500	1/16	50	300	27

FRACTION/DECIMAL/METRIC EQUIVALENTS

Fraction	Decimal	mm
1/64	0.015625	0.396875
1/32	0.031250	0.793750
3/64	0.046875	1.190625
1/16	0.062500	1.587500
5/64	0.078125	1.984375
3/32	0.093750	2.381250
7/64	0.109375	2.778125
1/8	0.125000	3.175000
9/64	0.140625	3.571875
5/32	0.156250	3.968750
11/64	0.171875	4.365625
3/16	0.187500	4.762500
13/64	0.203125	5.159375
7/32	0.218750	5.556250
15/64	0.234375	5.953125
1/4	0.250000	6.350000
17/64	0.265625	6.746875
9/32	0.281250	7.143750
19/64	0.296875	7.540625
5/16	0.312500	7.937500
21/64	0.328125	8.334375
11/32	0.343750	8.731250
23/64	0.359375	9.128125
3/8	0.375000	9.525000
25/64	0.390625	9.921875
13/32	0.406250	10.318750
27/64	0.421875	10.715625
7/16	0.437500	11.112500
29/64	0.453125	11.509375
15/32	0.468750	11.906250
31/64	0.484375	12.303125

Fraction/Decimal/Metric Equivalents

1/2	0.500000	12.700000
33/64	0.515625	13.096875
17/32	0.531250	13.493750
35/64	0.546875	13.890625
9/16	0.562500	14.287500
37/64	0.578125	14.684375
19/32	0.593750	15.081250
39/64	0.609375	15.478125
5/8	0.625000	15.875000
41/64	0.640625	16.271875
21/32	0.656250	16.668750
43/64	0.671875	17.065625
11/16	0.687500	17.462500
45/64	0.703125	17.859375
23/32	0.718750	18.256250
47/64	0.734375	18.653125
3/4	0.750000	19.050000
49/64	0.765625	19.446875
25/32	0.781250	19.843750
51/64	0.796875	20.240625
13/16	0.812500	20.637500
27/32	0.843750	21.431250
55/64	0.859375	21.828125
7/8	0.875000	22.225000
57/64	0.890625	22.621875
29/32	0.906250	23.018750
59/64	0.921875	23.415625
15/16	0.937500	23.812500
61/64	0.953125	24.209375
31/32	0.968750	24.606250
63/64	0.984375	25.003125
1.000000	1.000000	25.400000

DRILL SIZE SPECIFICATIONS

The drill bit is a tool used to cut and bore holes. The bits are available in many different sizes. Standards organizations have defined different sizes and sets that are made routinely by drill bit manufacturers and stocked by distributors. In the United States, fractional inch sizes such as ½ or ¼ are common. The following chart is a quick reference for specifications. The gauge number is a diameter dimension in millimeters. Sometimes you can use a digital dial caliper to measure the drill bit. The dial caliper converts the bit.

Drill size
Millimeter-Gauge-Fractional-Decimal Equivalencies

MM	Gauge	Frac.	Dec.	MM	Gauge	Frac.	Dec.	MM	Gauge	Frac.	Dec.	MM	Gauge	frac.	dec
	80		.0135	1.5			.0591		37		.1040	4.2			.1654
	79		.0145		53		.0595	2.7			.1063		19		.1660
		1/64	.0156	1.55			.0610		36		.1065	4.25			.1673
	78		.0160			1/16	.0625	2.75			.1083	4.3			.1693
	77		.0180	1.6			.0630			7/.64	.1093		18		.1695
	76		.0200		52		.0635		35		.1100			11/64	.1719
	75		.0210	1.65			.0650	2.8			.1102		17		.1730
	74		.0225	1.7			.0669		34		.1110	4.4			.1732
	73		.0240		51		.0670		33		.1130		16		.1770
	72		.0250	1.75			.0689	2.9			.1142	4.5			.1772
	71		.0260		50		.0700		32		.1160		15		.1800
	70		.0280	1.8			.0709	3.0			.1181	4.6			.1811
	69		.0292	1.85			.0728		31		.1200		14		.1820
	68		.0310		49		.0730	3.1			.1220	4.7	13		.1850
		1/32	.0313		48		.0760			1/8	.1225	4.75			.1870
	67		.0320	1.95			.0768	3.2			.1260			3/16	.1875
	66		.0330			5/64	.0781	3.25			.1280	4.8	12		.1890
	65		.0350		47		.0785		30		.1285		11		.1910
	64		.0360	2.0			.0787	3.3			.1299	4.9			.1929
	63		.0370	2.05			.0807	3.4			.1339		10		.1935
	62		.0380		46		.0810		29		.1360		9		.1960
	61		.0390		45		.0820	3.5			.1378	5.0			.1968
1.0			.0394	2.1			.0827		28		.1405		8		.1990
	60		.0400	2.15			.0846			9/64	.1406	5.1			.2008

Millimeter-Gauge-Fractional-Decimal Equivalencies

	59	.0410		44		.0860	3.6			.1417		7	13/64	.2010
1.05		.0413	2.2			.0866		27		.1440				.2031
	58	.0420	2.25			.0886	3.7			.1457		6		.2040
	57	.0430		43		.0890		26		.1470	5.2			.2047
1.1		.0433	2.3			.0906	3.75			.1476		5		.2055
1.15		.0455	2.35			.0925		25		.1495	5.25			.2067
	56	.0465		42		.0935	3.8			.1496	5.3			.2087
		.0469			3/32	.0937		24		.1520		4		.2090
1.2		.0472	2.4			.0945	3.9			.1535	5.4			.2126
1.25		.0492		41		.0960		23		.1540		3		.2130
1.3		.0512	2.45			.0965			5/32	.1562	5.5			.2165
	55	.0520		40		.0980		22		.1570			7/32	.2187
1.35		.0531	2.5			.0984	4.0			.1575	5.6			.2205
	54	.0550		39		.0995		21		.1590		2		.2210
1.4		.0551	2.6	38		.1015	4.1	20		.1610	5.7			.2244
1.45		.0571				.1024				.1614	5.75			.2264

Drill size
Millimeter-Gauge-Fractional-Decimal Equivalencies

MM	Gauge	Frac.	Dec.	MM	Gauge	Frac.	Dec.	MM	Gauge	Frac.	Dec.	MM	Gauge	Frac.	Dec.	MM	Gauge	Frac.	Dec.
	1		.2280		N		.3020	9.8			.3858							11/16	.6875
5.8			.2283	7.7			.3031		W		.3860	17.5							.6890
5.9			.2323	7.75			.3051	9.9			.3898							45/64	.7031
	A		.2340	7.8			.3071			25/64	.3906	18.0							.7087
		15/64	.2344	7.9			.3110	10.0			.3937							23/32	.7187
6.0			.2362			5/16	.3125		X		.3970	18.5							.7283
	B		.2380	8.0			.3150		Y		.4040							47/64	.7344
6.1			.2402		O		.3160			13/32	.4062	19.0							.7480
	C		.2420	8.1			.3189		Z		.4130							3/4	.7500
6.2			.2441	8.2			.3228	10.5			.4134							49/64	.7656
	D		.2460		P		.3230			27/64	.4219	19.5							.7677
6.25			.2461	8.25			.3248	11.0			.4331							25/32	.7812
6.3			.2480	8.3			.3268			7/16	.4375	20.0							.7874
		1/4	.2500			21/64	.3281	11.5			.4528							51/64	.7969
6.4			.2520	8.4			.3307			29/64	.4531	20.5							.8071
6.5			.2559		Q		.3320			15/32	.4687							13/16	.8025
	F		.2570	8.5			.3346	12.0			.4724	21.0							.8268
6.6			.2598	8.6			.3386			31/64	.4843							53/64	.8281
	G		.2610		R	11/32	.3390	12.5			.4921							27/32	.8437
6.7			.2638	8.7			.3425			1/2	.5000	21.5							.8465
		17/64	.2656				.3437	13.0			.5118							55/64	.8594
6.75			.2657	8.75			.3445			33/64	.5156	22.0							.8661
	H		.2660	8.8			.3465			18/32	.5313							7/8	.8750
6.8			.2677		S		.3480	13.5			.5315	22.5							.8858
6.9			.2717	8.9			.3504			35/64	.5469							57/64	.8906
	I		.2720	9.0			.3443	14.0			.5612	23.0							.9055
7.0			.2756		T		.3580			9/16	.5625							29/32	.9062
	J		.2770	9.1			.3583	14.5			.5709							59/64	.9219
7.1			.2795			23/64	.3594			37/64	.5781	23.5							.9252
	K		.2811	9.2			.3622	15.0			.5906							15/16	.9375
		9/32	.2812	9.25			.3642			19/32	.5937	24.0							.9449
7.2			.2835	9.3			.3661			39/64	.6094							61/64	.9531
7.25			.2854		U		.3680	15.5			.6102	24.5							.9546

Millimeter-Gauge-Fractional-Decimal Equivalencies

7.3			.2874	9.4			.3701		5/8	.6250			31/32	.9687
	L		.2900	9.5			.3740	16.0		.6299				.9843
7.4			.2913			3/8	.3750		41/64	.6406			63/64	.9844
	M		.2950		V		.3770	16.5		.6496			1"	1.000
7.5			.2953	9.6			.3780		21/32	.6562				
		19/64	.2968	9.7			.3819	17.7		.6693				
7.6			.2992	9.75			.3839		43/64	.6719				

DRILL AND TAP METRICS

*ISO (Metric) Sizes

Fastener size mm	Coarse Threads		Fine Threads	
	Pitch	Drill	Pitch	Threads
1.4	.3	1.1		
1.6	.35	1.25		
2.	.4	1.6		
2.5	.45	2.05		
3	.5	2.5		
4	.7	2.3		
5	.8	4.2		
6	1	5		
8	1.25	6.75	1	7
10	1.5	8.5	1.25	8.75
12	1.75	10.25	1.25	10.50
14	2	12	1.5	12.5
16	2	14	1.5	14.5
18	2.5	15.5	1.5	16.5
20	2.5	17.5	1.5	18.5
22	2.5	19.5	1.5	20.5
24	3	21	2	22
27	3	24	2	25

Pitch in ISO is the number of millimeters between the peaks of the threads.

*International Organization for Standardization
Drill and Tap Metric
Coarse Thread

Thread Size—UNC	Drill Diameter	Tap Drill Size
1-64	.0595	No. 53
2-56	.0700	No. 50
3-48	.0785	No. 47
4-40	.0890	No. 43
5-40	.1015	No. 38
6-32	.1065	No. 36
8-32	.1360	No. 29
10-24	.1495	No. 25
12-24	.1770	No. 16
1/4-20	.2010	No. 7
5/16-18	.2570	'F'
3/8-16	.3125	5/16
7/16-14	.3680	'U'
1/2-13	.4219	27/64
9/16-12	.4844	31/64
5/8-11	.5312	17/32
3/4-10	.6562	21/32
7/8-9	.7656	49/64
1"-8	.8750	7/8

Fine Thread

Thread Size—UNF	Drill Diameter	Tap Drill Size
0-80 UNF	.0469	3/64
1-72 UNF	.0595	No. 53
2-64 UNF	.0700	No. 50
3-56 UNF	.0820	No. 45
4-48 UNF	.0935	No. 42
5-44 UNF	.1040	No. 37
6-40 UNF	.1130	No. 33
8-36 UNF	.1360	No. 29
10-32 UNF	.1590	No. 21
12-28 UNF	.1820	No. 14
1/4-28 UNF	.2130	No. 3
5/16-24 UNF	.2720	'I'
3/8-24 UNF	.3320	'Q'
7/16-20 UNF	.3906	25/64
1/2-20 UNF	.4531	29/64
9/16-18 UNF	.5156	33/64
5/8-18 UNF	.5781	37/64
3/4-16 UNF	.6875	11/16
7/8-14 UNF	.8125	13/16
1"-14 UNF	.9375	59/64

CPSIA information can be obtained at www.ICGtesting.com
Printed in the USA
BVOW03s0022160215

387651BV00019B/36/P